A Field Guide to the Heavens

The Brittingham Prize in Poetry

The University of Wisconsin Press Poetry Series
Ronald Wallace, General Editor

FRANK X. GASPAR

A Field Guide

to the

Heavens

THE UNIVERSITY OF WISCONSIN PRESS

The University of Wisconsin Press
2537 Daniels Street
Madison, Wisconsin 53718

3 Henrietta Street
London WC2E 8LU, England

Library of Congress Cataloging-in-Publication-Data
Gaspar, Frank X.
A field guide to the heavens / Frank X. Gaspar.
96 pp. cm.—(The Brittingham prize in poetry)
ISBN 0-299-16520-5 (cloth: alk. paper)
ISBN 0-299-16524-8 (pbk.: alk. paper)
I. Title. II. Series: Brittingham prize in poetry (Series)
PS3557.A8448F54   1999
811'.54—dc21   99-15687

He created seven heavens, one above the other. You will not see a flaw in the Merciful's creation. Turn up your eyes: can you detect a crack?

THE KORAN

The great anguishes of the soul always come upon us like cosmic cataclysms. When they do, the sun errs from its course and all the stars are troubled.

FERNANDO PESSOA

CONTENTS

III. This Small Book of Days

ACKNOWLEDGMENTS

Grateful acknowledgment is made to the editors of the following magazines and anthologies where these poems originally appeared:

Bellingham Review: "A Spell Against Ruin," "What Good Are the Stars"
Broad River: "First Epistle in June," "I Am Refused Entry to the Harvard Poetry Library," "Part of What I Mean"
Double Take: "February," "The Lemons"
Georgia Review: "The Fire and the Rose," "Seven Roses"
Gettysburg Review: "When Lilacs"
Harvard Review: "Dream Talk"
Kenyon Review: "A Field Guide to the Heavens," "The Tree," "Whiskey," "Confessions," "Small Prayer for the World Without Mercy on Us," "Kapital"
Massachusetts Review: "George Herbert"
Pearl: "Now the Moon Is in the First Quarter"
Ploughshares: "Education by Stone," "The Lilies of the Field"
Prairie Schooner: "Shook Foil," "An Ark Cast into the Flags"
Quarterly West: "Last Hymn to Night"
Tampa Review: "A Witness Gives His Version," "This Small Book of Days"

Best American Poetry 1996 (Scribners): "Kapital"
Urban Nature (Milkweed Editions): "Part of What I Mean," "The Tree"

The author wishes to thank the National Endowment for the Arts and the California Arts Council for fellowships which aided in the completion of this book.

I

Metropolis

He was conscious of two rhythms that were slowly becoming one. When they became one, his identification with God was complete. His heart was the one heart, the heart of God. And his brain was likewise God's.

God said, "Will you accept it now?"

And he replied, "I accept, I accept."

NATHANIEL WEST, *Miss Lonelyhearts*

A Field Guide to the Heavens

Tonight I am speaking in tongues again.
Listen to all the stars with names as old as Mesopotamia:
Rukbat, Arkab, Nunki, Lesath, Shaula. They are shining forth
in the Archer and the Scorpion. They are ablaze in the southern sky.
The Scorpion rests his tail on some trees and a streetlight. Now and then
when I go inside to warm some coffee or toast some bread, I read
a few snatches of Milton, who laments death as the loss of intellect,
who says, *Are not the towers of heaven filled with armed watch?*
I am looking for certain signs, certain deliriums. This Scorpion
is the same that stung mighty Orion to death. This Archer
pursues him for all eternity, in his left hand the bow, in his right,
the flaming arrow. This region is rich and manifold. In this direction
lies the center of our galaxy, a holy fire. *Aloof the vulgar constellations thick,*
says Milton, and I walk outside again. The ducks over in the park
are raving mad. Their sounds float on the night wind. The neighbors sleep
in one another's arms. Listen: *Dschubba, Antares, Acrab.* What
are they saying in the aisles and naves of the light years? What
is the sacred word on the street? What celestial music am I
so afraid to miss? In my right hand there is nothing. In my left
hand there is a cup. In my short chair in the shadows I am invisible.
This is how I know my street is a garden and my yard is a bower.
My coffee cools in the slow breeze. Someone's cat circles,
curious, lets me touch the scruff of its neck before it goes off to hunt
for meat or sex. The shrubs and trees and flowers all become
one another's equals in the slow eyes of darkness. *Sing,*
heavenly Muse, says Milton. *Geidi, Nashira, Dabih.* Eat
every fruit, sleep soundly: surely, verily, nothing will be lost.

Dog Days

So called because Sirius, the dog star,
rises again in this month, something I'm told
many do not know. I don't look for it.
I prefer to wait until it is high in the night
chasing Orion, who chases the Bull, when
the weather is cool and the nights are long.
Now I am in the muggy room under a light.
Now I am ignorant, continually losing my way.
I have been to a part of the world where people
put *The Teaching of Buddha* in hotel room drawers.
I brought one home—a handsome cheap copy, hardback.
I believe it was meant to be. I am reading all the left-hand pages,
which are English. On the right is Chinese, long
strips of exquisite characters that would not appear to mean
anything, but which I accept on faith. I have dog-eared
many pages already, but the one I come back to is
the Buddha's list of twenty difficult things. *It is hard*
not to desire things that are beautiful and attractive,
he says. *It is hard to apply oneself to study widely*
and thoroughly. It is hard not to despise the beginner.
I do not know what is happening to me. Everything
is green and shaggy and robust. At night I can hear
the wet grass in its dark ecstasies, I can hear the citrus
buds humming the small pains of their multiform births.
Surely I am not calm or wise, surely small flames whisper
from the fissures in my head, surely my eyes are burning like
cheap candles. Something is trying to convince me that I will
go on like this forever, and I am ready to shout and believe it.
When you look behind the stars, there are more stars.
When you walk out in the August night and ask yourself
where you are going in all this wilderness of waves and particles,
you hear everything answering at once, so clear, so mysterious.
That's when you walk in circles lamenting how little you know.

That's when you strike off in every direction at once.
It's your own mind, says the Buddha, *that causes pain,*
grief, lamentation, delusion. It's hard, says the Buddha,
to be born while Buddha is in the world.

Metropolis

I'm doing nothing.
All over the west side cars are warming up.
Tonight the evening star is Jupiter, big
as a chunk of glass, near a waning moon.
Nothing else in the sky shows through
except the running lights on the liners
vectoring into LAX. I'm not thinking
about anything fancy, nothing post-
modern, no *desire*, no *difference,* but
my friend and I have lugged the pieces
of the telescope out of the garage, and
we horsed the big tube onto the frame
and stopped the aperture down, and
now he's at the eyepiece watching the
four moons in their quiet dance around
that indifferent world. We've got some good
bourbon and two cups. I know how
to measure and predict the transit
of the moons, track their shadows on
the spotted surface, time occultations,
but we're doing nothing, just watching
the silence out there, the ice, the gravity,
and we're talking, and of course there
were the shootings on the west side, always
the shootings because of the two rival
gangs, though we can't make out exactly
what's what from the newspaper, and
I'm telling him about my student, out
of jail, born-again, second string tailback
on the football team, of all things, and
he's in jail again, this time a terrible bust,
drunk at a party, the gangster thing again,
and he stabs a boy to death over an in-

sult to somebody's girlfriend, not even
his own. He was shy, I tell my friend,
and his smile would loosen up the room—
his skin was black as iron, and cornrows,
and arms like barrels—everybody liked him.
The neighborhood squats under the sky-
glow—too much city light, too much smog.
The woman one house over opens her door
and shoos a cat out onto the lawn. The
girl across the street sits on her step
talking to her boyfriend, high school stuff,
so serious, so much feeling. Now I'm
at the eyepiece, nudging the barrel,
following Jupiter and its moons. *Io* has
disappeared behind the planet's disk,
and *Europa, Callisto,* and *Ganymede* waltz
in space, perfect jewels, points gleaming
in far sunshine. My friend is pensive
now, jotting in his notebook in the dark.
The bourbon is warm and sweet in
the aluminum cup. This is what I want
tonight. This is just about right. I'm
not thinking about anything fancy.
I'm doing just about nothing.

Now the Moon Is in the First Quarter

Now the moon is in the first quarter.
It hangs above my house, crisp and bruised.
Now the moonlight is significant, pulling me outside
to live with the insects and the small animals.
Behind some loose bricks near the garden wall
a cricket is making noises with her tempered legs. Everywhere
the smell of night-blooming jasmine drifts and sleeps.
The siren off in the boulevard is calling out one of the names of God,
and across the street my neighbor sits on his front steps, smoking.
He has been fighting with his wife for weeks. He doesn't see me yet.
When he flips his cigarette into the street, the orange coal bursts
into a little galaxy of sparks. His silence holds
the stars in silence. All around us there are so many hungers:
I know the places in the park where people lie hidden
next to their bags of worldly possessions. I know
the places where one must never walk.
I have to set the record straight. I have to get
one or two things exactly right even though I know
that I am only blood and dirt. Now I can
sit on the cool concrete of my own steps
and smile and nod at the Creation, although
I understand next to nothing. Sometimes
on nights just like this one, my street becomes
a glistening river, and you can go down to it and put
your hands into it, and the waters of your life
will wash over your disasters. Then the stars
will work hard for you. Then the small bats
will tattoo a celebration around the streetlights.
Then you can rest without sorrow behind my juniper hedge.
Then you can tell me what it is that *I* must do.

The Tree

Then God said to me, *stop*
feeling sorry for yourself—isn't it
enough that I love you? But I was
angry and sleepy in that indistinct way
when dreams linger like a fog in your head
all morning long, and I went out
to the work I grudged: God wanted me
to walk through the garden naming things,
but the wind was coming off the ocean six
miles down the boulevard, and a mockingbird
sat on the roof painting the whole house with
polyphonies, and then the finches and
the gray doves and the parkway crows
began lighting up the eaves and the canopies,
and then God told me to be humble, so I trellised
the sweet peas and hosed the spall and whitefly
from the citrus leaves, and I was thinking
the whole time about love, how so many live
and die without it, and what that must mean,
but God rebuked me and bade me wrestle
with the tree, so I took the saw and hatchet
down to the narrow place along the neighbor's
cinder blocks and prepared to cut and hack,
as I do each spring, this anonymous tree
that sends out its runners, and God said,
that tree will strangle your roses and
smite your false heather—
left alone it will crack the sidewalk
and rise up waving and whistling, and so I
attacked the saplings that had sprung up
window-high and wrist-thick along
its buried roots, and I chopped and I
sawed, and the leaves shivered green and gray

in the morning light, and a shower of small
orange moths burst up like hands dancing
all around my head, and I looked at them
and saw how they moved in the world, like
light bouncing from shadow to shadow,
and I saw their terror.

I Work Late at My Table in Summer

June bugs are hurling their fat, homely bodies
at the pale light in my doorways. Sometimes
I go to the back steps, where they have piled up
under the lightbulb like a kind of snow, and
I run my hands through them. They are
aloof and driven and free of any malice.
Sometimes they drop against the windows like pennies,
so dull and copper, and I am pleased to see them,
for now, in the order of things, the mockingbird
can stop singing for sex, and the jacarandas
will know it's time for casting off their royal favors.
I am at the table then with paper and something
to mark it with. I am breathing the same air, the same
late hour. I am thinking about how Blake nailed
the question. It's not *if God*, but *what does all
the silence mean?* Who knows what the june bugs
listen to. Mars is up, red and strong, swaggering
into Virgo, fog bells are banging out in the far
channels where the stone barges lie at anchor,
a train whistle burrows deep in the west side.
All over the city, creatures are devout and full of purpose,
and now these small ones, bumbling and flying, ignoring
their failures. Let them tap and fluster in their
pill bodies. Let them roll and cleave on their
spindle legs. The porchlights and streetlights
are all their happiness, and my windows, where
they are a soft rain, where I don't draw the blinds,
where I don't douse the hungry lamp.

First Epistle in June

For days now the wind has freshened off the beach
and scoured the airport and the stadium and the avenues,
and cooled the composition roof and the stucco walls,
and dandled the iron chimes on the verandah and
wreathed the moon with vapors: For days
I have waited for signs, I have read the old books,
I have listened for news from behind my bellying curtains,
behind my nodding roses. For nights I've stayed awake
counting, trying to drive a stake into the old myths, trying
to see the world in a natural light. For nights I have sat
amazed at all the dangers, so sudden in this calm life,
and after so many small, mean lives of peril behind me.
I confess I am bewildered in the true sense of a *wildness*.
Sometimes this very street looks perfect, deep in
the deep hours, when the trash containers are lined
precisely at the curbs, and the old newspapers are stacked
for the recyclers under modest bricks and stones, and
the automobiles grin like fattened animals in the false lights
and the true lights. But you can't let yourself be fooled
by these plankton breezes and blackened streets. I've gone out
myself along the rows of houses. I've walked to the edges
of the park where the owl lives and the crows in the tall pines.
It's like watching sand run through a pinched glass: everything
is turning into language, and you can't keep still despite yourself.
I'm telling you this freely. I've sat on the sidewalk
and parsed the gladiolus and the poppy and felt the heat
go out of the earth like a long sleep. Not one of us is safe.

July in the Street of Fevers

In July I am nothing but streetlight—
it's another month of no rain and early fogs blowing in.
I have by heart each stop of the moon, every signal star.
Under my right hand I have four hundred and eighty-eight poems.
I have discovered how foolish it is to ever sleep.
All over the neighborhood weeds and graffiti are speaking
their free language against law and order: even my plum tree
gives forth a sharp ticking from under its soft bark.
Some houses have fans turning in the windows and a
parchment light glowing through blinds or curtains.
In one house a woman has moved her hospital bed
into the living room, and she leaves the drapes open
to let the orange night-lights gleam against the stainless steel.
No one geranium or bicycle sits quietly without its four narratives.
The people on my street will give you a cup of sugar or
an egg if you ask for it. They like a little gossip, too.
They want to hear stories about work and love. They are
unaware of all the official postures. They like to know
how things connect. They've all seen me one night or another
roaming the street, sometimes without my body, one house,
two houses, three houses down the block. If they asked me
I'd tell them I was out looking for the Buddha of the Blue Galaxies
or Jehovah of the Mu Meson, and those would be stories, too.
But no one ever complains. When we meet in the world of light,
they show me a civil kindness. They nod and smile or wave.
They know I am the one who sets the dogs to barking, but
no one lets on that they know. No one says a thing.

Psalms in August

Because I walk among husks and shadows,
I am afraid for my own soul. I don't know
what *soul* means except as I read the Greeks,
and I read them in English because of my chronic ignorance.
Now that the storms have passed and the heat has blown by
in exalted, fish-scaled clouds, we can open the house
again at night. The city has grown tired of its own summer.
It wants a rest. It has become quiet and civil, though two
dogs are barking in backyards on another street. They
seem to be answering one another. They are so pure
that they can only lament or praise. They are both
low and high, both rich and poor together. They
remind me to chronicle how I live, late in the millennium,
with two glass doors on the back of my house, and a
wooden porch with four chairs on it, where we sometimes
sit and drink Mexican beer with limes. Sometimes I
sit there and talk with my friend who believes that God
died in the Big Bang, a sacrifice to make the world, and
that is why we can only guess at traces of Him. He believes
that this is at the bottom of the mystery. He wears *Mi Vida
Loca* tattooed across the small of his back. He wants
to know if Allen Ginsberg got the title *Howl* from reading
Rimbaud's *A Season in Hell.* My friend spent a small part
of the summer under suicide watch in a local hospital, but
he has managed lately to evade his despair. You have to be
crazy not to be so afraid of God that you are crazy. When
I am happiest, I am most afraid, but being happy I do not
pay attention to the fear. All my instruments are out
of tune, and my hands are no longer suited for music,
which I was permitted to only love from a distance. But
I would call the Chief Musician, if I could. I would sing,

if I could, like those dogs, who are not yet annoying
the proper citizens. Just like my friend and me, the dogs
might be happy that something has saved them with its right hand.
Just like us, they might be drinking the wine of astonishment.

The Lemons

Forget the sun and the dizzy moths.
Forget the pieces of mockingbird that the cats have left by the side gate.
Forget the hose running under the honeysuckle:
the lemons are offering us holiness again.
They are making us go down on our knees to smell them.
They are making us think of our old loves, to grieve over them.
They are singing every little song, they are conjuring every temptation.
They have been having sex with the oranges and tangerines, the yard
is rife with their pollens, they are sweeter than they even know.
They speak together. They are amazing me with their navels and nipples.
How they flaunt themselves on the spider-veined limbs all pained with thorn.
They are trying to make me lazy, to turn me against my simple work—
they do not want to be plucked from their own dreaming.
They are telling us again how they come each year, bringing secrets
from their other world, and how we are never able to decipher them.
How long now before we put up the aluminum ladder
and pull on the leather-palmed gloves? How long with the shape
and heft of lemon voluptuous in my hand? How long
with the summer in its steep track, and the low cars cruising
out on the avenues, and the drone of the small airplanes
like bees over the far houses?

George Herbert

I am watching the morning stars sing together.
In this case they make up *The Sickle,* the asterism
of Leo's head, angling down over the vacant house
across the street and four doors down. At this hour,
in the steep dark of morning, when even the city lights
have dwindled down to the lonely and the terrible,
these stars are bold and odd. They make a certain claim,
and I can be happy, talking to myself without disturbing
the silence of the black lawns and sidewalks. Now
is the time for a wider eyepiece to rove the shelves
of galaxies under Leo's belly. Now is the time to
reckon with George Herbert, who mentions stars
too many times to count, and moons and spheres
and the *fleet astronomer.* George Herbert, whose
lines are too beautiful for the intellect, who will never
leave your mind at rest once you've let him in. His
mind runs perpendicular to my own: he is uncomfortable
with the telescope, but he is fascinated by it. He
compares the faint nebulas to moths. We are so alone,
finally: it is like walking through a curtain of danger
and sitting, breathing hard, on its far side. Nothing
was truly as difficult as we imagined. I nudge the
barrel of the scope and find a galactic reef that never
stops diminishing. This darkness will not last forever,
we have to make the most of it before the sky lightens
and the neighbors begin rising to the day. Soon a car
will come around the corner and someone will throw
a copy of the *Times* at our feet. The truth is that
I never want to leave here. The truth is that we might
strike an accommodation, though neither of us can
imagine what it might be. I can't dispute what is holy—
I can't dispute his decision to lament and love.
But here, look, I show him how I sweep the sky,

slowly, slowly, back and forth, how to come upon
something obliquely, unexpected, at first just a wisp,
a figment, but then holding it, shimmering at the edge
of seeing, like an idea you can't quite pull into focus,
that faint gauze, that *almost-nothing* that is a whole world.

Seven Roses

Three red, one white, one purple, one yellow, one pink.
Seven roses in a jar on the kitchen table, the morning
paper, Kona coffee, a plate of sliced melon and banana.
I'm in a fogbank. I was out wandering the keeps
of some mind or another far too late. Now all I can do
is stare at the roses, which smell wonderful, as does
the fruit, as does the coffee. The truth about life is
that it is good, but it comes with a lot of strings attached.
The rose bushes were here when we bought
this house, though we have added to them, subtracted
from them. Frankly, I don't like them much. They
demand so much of you. They want to be fertilized
and pruned and mulched. Then they get sick, they
get rusty and moldy, and things live in them and you
must resort to despicable substances, you have to
wear yellow gloves. All that time out in the heat
when you could be bodysurfing or reading a book.
If I were Rumi I could make a parable about the roses,
I could dance into a fainting spell and someone on my staff
would write down the poem I uttered, or if I were Francis Ponge
I could study the roses in a way that a cubist might,
just before painting them all up and down a stretched canvas.
I've looked at the hard truth: that my heart might be just
too dark for roses. Or my soul too weary. Or my mind
too confused. Yet they *are* beautiful here in their cut
ripeness, their delicate bowing to earth. See how the air
beads into water all along the jar. And the white rose,
its delicate, almost invisible kiss of red at the edges of
its inner petals. It is all so strange in the morning when
I cannot think, and when my body at rest wishes to remain
at rest, which is the law, after all. I know it's the way
of the world that the roses and I have so much to do
with one another. It's one hand washing the other hand.

It's morning and I take to the day slowly, grow
into my senses slowly. And maybe the roses puzzle after me in
their fashion, the seven lovely roses sitting on my table,
scenting the sunlit room. Maybe they know that I know
how they hate the way they are softly, softly dying for me.

I See Men but They Look Like Trees Walking

I walk the five small blocks from here, heading
north, and hit the park, which runs like a ribbon
for miles and miles along the boulevard. I wind among
the cement bicycle paths to the pond, and I stop and admire
the piñatas and the pick-up soccer games and the sweet
smells of pork and marijuana. I turn my head from the lovers
who have nowhere else to go, and I shift my eyes from
the shirtless boys in their tattoos and shaved heads, who sit
on the long stone tables in silence. I watch three old men
fish for carp in the brown water. I try to speak with the woman
whose home is an old Radio Flyer wagon and seven coats. I am
trying to be very careful, very precise. I am resisting the current
pressures to despair of depths and surfaces. I'm trying to render
unto Caesar and turn the other cheek. I slip into the library
and come out with an armload of books when the sun is breaking
into loaves and fishes in the long, significant limbs of the trees.
I want to ask George Herbert a question where someone has check-
marked a page and circled his name in blue ink. I thumb through
a small book on a new drug for the mind and turn back a corner
of one page to come back to later. I am trying not to be stuck in
my old ways. I am trying not to love my own pride and ignorance.
I am always getting drunk on what someone else has said: All these people.
All these minds working. I see a woman all in green, glowing
like some rare element, running under her black headphones,
I see a skinny man with a cigarette kick a fat duck. I am trying to keep
things simple. I see men and women walking at the far edge of the grass,
backlit and throwing long shadows. Just like you, I can't tell what they are.

Last Hymn to Night

divinest Melancholy
—Milton

Let the house sleep.
    Let the city carry on its restless percussions,
let the urban possums raid the fruits of my lemon trees,
      let my driveway
reflect the pumice shine of the moon.
      Let the dead speak in the one way I know
and let me be listening.
        Let me be strong
now that the weak are sleeping and saving themselves,
      for like you, I'm moving beyond
            love and hope.
I think you know what I mean:
    Let there be coffee, dark and simple
         in the blue mug on the many-ringed desk,
and whisky neat in the short glass among
    the clutter of books and stacks of paper,
and the long, dangerous pencils, and the machine
         for writing.
    Let the cut grass whimper under the snails' track,
      let the neighbor's cat thud on the roof, let
the lamp burn from my window in yellow warning
      that sometimes
I will spill through a crack in the door
    and hunch in shadows tying numbers to stars
in the blunt metropolitan sky.
    Let me forget there will be a time for my silence:
      Let me just remember how the jacarandas look
        wreathed in night-fog, the sodium glow
of streetlight striking halos in their branches, let
    the heaters kick on with their quiet thump,

let the distant thrum of the refrigerator
suddenly cease and plunge us into the vatic world:
   Let me turn at the mill, let me make
  the small breathing sounds of rapture and effort,
shaking off the day's dust and loathing,
      let me reach into
the quailing language of the room and find a heartbeat,
  let me fill the black slate of the neighborhood
    with stems and serifs,
  let the night spawn orisons everywhere—
I think you know what I mean:
  Let the mockingbirds whistle dementia in the chimney.
Let the far dogs moan like fence posts in the wind.
   Let the jasmine bloom.

II

Jailhouse Tattoos

If a church made by human beings can be full of symbols,
how much more full must the universe be. It is infinitely full of
them. We must read into them.

SIMONE WEIL

To be a poet in a destitute time means to attend, singing, to
the trace of the fugitive gods. This is why the poet in the time
of the world's night utters the holy. This is why the world's
night is the holy night.

MARTIN HEIDEGGER

The Fire and the Rose

Some days are meant to be filled with shame
and misgiving. Now I'm breathless, sitting
at the table waiting for the sun to come up or
for the kettle to boil or for my joints to stop aching.
I would like permission to write poems, to love
George Herbert without saying a single smart thing
about him, to hate some of the Psalms
and most of Leviticus and Deuteronomy. I need a rest.
I have come too close to seeing a place where
the fire and the rose are one. I can tell you
that no one comes back. I can tell you
we are all headed in the same direction. Last night
my beloved was weary, and I rubbed her bones. One
friend is losing a breast, and so is another. One
night the house was filled with women.
I had nowhere to go and so locked myself
in a small room with books. But the house was loud.
It never stopped whooping and talking and laughing.
Then I was in a desert of great beauty and I heard
wisdom. It sounded like laughter and talking and
whooping. I crept to the edge of the circle of firelight
and tried to understand that host of brilliant creatures there.
Maybe they would devour me. Maybe
they would drive me away. It didn't matter.
I never came in from the darkness.
I kept to my cloak of inconsequence. When the sun
came up there were only signs and memory.
I found the print of one naked foot, perfect
in the rough sand. I thought I would lift it in my hands
and take it back with me as a talisman.
I thought about it night after night after night
as the stars wheeled over me, as I told myself
that this, or something like this, would be possible.

A Spell Against Ruin

this journey upon which I go with thee

I am reading Dante, late at night, trying
to get him to speak to me. I want to know
what he means about the venality of the Popes,
and I want to know why Beatrice laments
the lack of right government. I want to know
what this has to do with me, why Dante
has written these things particularly to me,
and how he means me to save myself with them.
My clocks are all off. No two of them point
to the same time, and at this hour of night
the big cheap blue clock on the kitchen wall
ticks out loud, the second hand lurching
forward, around and around: it was Wittgenstein
who said we can't measure time, only one process
against another. This is simple to understand
until you consider its implications. I don't
believe Dante is dead in any sense of the word,
and I don't know why he has picked *me* to receive
his guidance and unstring his ciphers. I have
been drinking supermarket wine and eating
potato chips. I have committed a number
of sins which Dante doesn't specifically
catalogue, and I'm thinking that he might
have been wrong in his ideas of punishment.
I'm thinking that sins somehow are ruin in
themselves, and you can test this by examining
your own life. I have not taken myself seriously
enough—I know this much. I don't have the time
that I used to have, either. Sometimes I still want
to take out my flattop guitar, the most
lovely thing I have ever owned, and I want

to play it so that when I am finished, my fingers
will smell like the brass windings on the three
bass strings. But I don't. There's so much
to be done that I don't dare test my joints in
that way anymore. *So I say to Dante:*
Let me proceed to that second realm which
purifies man's spirit of its soilure. I'm ready
to put aside my anger and my vanity, and
I'm ready to entertain the dead and to treat
them politely. I know you are trying to tell
me something when you speak about the centaurs
shooting arrows at the damned. I know terrible
things about love. I have made many mistakes.
I know that if I read you at a certain hour in a certain
light in a certain sequence, you will yield up a spell
against ruin. After all these wasted years, I am
finally willing to declaim myself. I am all yours.
I am willing to hold the book any way you wish.

September Tropical

This must be the blue period.
Everyone is talking about the warm current
building off the shores of Peru and Chile.
When I go down to the beach in the early hours,
the sea is rolling like oil. One or two longboarders
sit out along the jetty on the smooth water, waiting.
I can smell the weed, the mussels, the kelp, the salt.
I can smell the coffee brewing in the little window
by the boathouse where a Vietnamese woman
sells muffins from dawn to whenever.
Everybody I talk to is finally afraid to sleep.
I don't ask what they do all night long. I am
out in the gray streaks of morning sifting among
the theories. Sometimes I find a shell or two,
or some smoothed glass. Strange fish are jumping
all over the harbor—even the newspapers tell us about it.
I am not convinced that virtue lies between two extremes,
but that's what I'm considering as I wax my board. I
should be doing other things. I should be carrying
my share of the burden. On the other hand, I forgive
myself for everything. I forgive almost everyone else, too,
even the ones who try to tell me that I'm just stuck
in language, *that* old idea, the fog lying over the fog.
When the channel bell strikes, I paddle out to the break
and wait for something shapely. Sure, my fingers
hurt a little in the chilly water, my knees, my elbows,
but it's a small price because I plan to get somewhere. A set
builds and I let the first wave go under me, round and
friendly. I let the second one go, too, but the third
swell is the big brother, and I stroke out and turn
into position, then paddle, paddle. This is how
to get to where the world topples beyond good and evil,
beneath all the mysteries, to where nothing *means.* Try it.

If the pelicans fly over you and terrify you with the pure
rapacious appetite in their eyes, you can forgive them.
If a harbor seal stands off looking like a channel buoy
in the mist and spray, forgive his strangeness. In
the meantime when that dune of water rises beneath you,
blue and glassy and dangerous, and utterly without mind,
I believe your head will be filled with bliss and confusion.
For you will be lifted up. For you will be thrown down.

Among the Quadi, on the River Gran

Tonight it's Marcus Aurelius. Tonight the lights
are flickering and fading from a great strain on the electrical
grid: All over the city, fans and air-conditioners are whining
in the heat, and the saffron air is buffed with the wind of cars
motoring out on the broad streets that run from the ocean to
the graves of the fruit orchards. How can I read Marcus Aurelius
and think of the little room I lived in back in Manhattan when
I was seventeen and far from home? How can I read him
and think of the night two policemen handcuffed that man
to the chain-link fence in the alley and beat the living shit
out of him—and my friend, who was AWOL from the army,
and I four floors up watched from the one dark window?
That's when I needed Marcus Aurelius to save me from
my ignorance and anger. Oh, if he had been with me. Oh,
the lives I wasted simply because I wanted so much and
knew so little. How I needed maxims, examples, laws!
I loved that city, but I couldn't make sense of it.
I didn't know how to get at its poems. I couldn't
find its art. Now it's too late to make amends. Now I just
read Marcus Aurelius in the heat, sentence after sentence,
afraid to stop. I drink a little whisky. I drink a little coffee.
I dog-ear a page and then another and another. I think
I may be a narcissist the way I read Marcus Aurelius and
think only of myself. Certainly I am agitated. I have fallen
into my obsessions, and I have to admit I feel something
like ecstasy. Sometimes I simply feel dread. Sometimes my
breath comes in sharp heaves when I think I see myself
in the pulpy text: *an exile, self-banished from the polity
of reason,* or *a limb lopped from the community!* Well, I can't
be everyone's friend. I haven't even reached the moral law yet.
I don't know when I'll get there. Maybe never. The night
is eerie, so silent except for machines. The insects, the birds,
the crawling things have all disappeared into their remedies

for temperature: the appliances buzz and hum, my lamp
every so often stutters like a murmuring heart, the fans
sing little hymns. It doesn't matter. I am with Marcus
Aurelius now. The campaign is going well. Perhaps
there is still some time left to meditate, to consider.
A man must have a point of view. We find we resemble
one another somewhat, especially our noses. We run our
fingers through our thick beards. We take up many problems,
and he turns them around and around in his stalwart mind.
The river winds through green rushes. It has taken so long
to get here. In a tent somewhere down the line a voice is breathing
a tiresome song of sorrow and regret, and the heat is oppressive,
but when one is prepared in his soul, such things become trivial.

The Apostle Paul Disappears into a Crowd at Corinth

It must have been Corinth or perhaps Ephesus,
the gray day and the gray marble of the public buildings
and the gray beards—everything like a muted photograph
in an old textbook, and I wanted to catch his eye,
but by the look on his face he seemed busily occupied
in his own mind, and he turned before I could call out to him:
I wanted to shout, *Damascus!* I wanted to shout, *James!*
I wanted to corner him and examine him once and for all,
for I had traveled a long way with him constantly in my thoughts,
and I was angry and felt I had been ill-used.
Yes, it was definitely Corinth, I could tell by the crowns
on the columns of the porches. It was dusty and the streets
were bustling the way you often see in movies when
the director wants to establish something ancient,
something exotic, something beyond your own experience
but presented to you in the *terms* of your experience so
that nothing is quite real, yet you are supplied with *context*.
This would be Corinth. It was a remarkable city with
narrow streets and stucco buildings garlanded with wisteria
and bougainvillea, not unlike our own neighborhoods.
Paul could have been a neighbor out walking, looking
up and down the street for the mail carrier in the late afternoon.
The lawns of Corinth greened under their small fountains.
Palm trees arched slowly into the reddish air. I came
this close to catching Paul. I took my eye off him for
a second and he was gone, slipped through my fingers,
my only chance. I would not have gone easy on him.
You can't say, for instance, *This birth of mine was monstrous*
and then just glide away like a car in traffic. You can't
talk to practical Greeks about raising the dead, you can't
talk in circles about belief. And those Ephesian books
going up in flames! How familiar is Corinth now
that evening settles. The stars are feeble and intimate.

Paul is somewhere out there among the lighted windows.
Perhaps he sits at a table writing letters. Maybe his shadow
flutters on the wall when the breeze strikes his candle.
Maybe he gets up to shoo a cat from his roses. I came
so close. I would have settled every question. I would
have pressed my suspicions. You would have to feel
sorry for him, really, for he would be no match for me:
I have spent too many hours learning his mind, which
after all, I discovered is the same as my mind: He
will tell you anything, he will stop at nothing.
You can hear the waves breaking on the shores of Corinth,
and far in the high hills something drones, so amazingly
like the sound of an airplane or a distant freeway. *Paul
has escaped.* He is stroking his beard and plotting. He
is hiding among the market-goers, pushing his shopping
cart and chanting syllables from the Temple. You can
catch the glimmer of some inexplicable light shimmering
off his garment. I know he's there. I raise my
hands to my lips to shout, but then it's too late.
He has ducked his head. He has turned the corner.

An Ark Cast into the Flags

Today there is rolling thunder at the beach.
The multitudes have come to watch, with their cameras
and their bright clothes. Cars and vans choke the streets.
The tanned boys are all gristle and sinew carrying their boards.
The storm surf is rolling up from nineteen-hundred miles off Baja,
and it rounds the pier like hills and hills, going out to the horizon.
The curls clap the sand and shake the earth, the air is all foam
and spray and mist. A television crew has set up its equipment.
The riders sit respectfully on the sand and meditate the shapes,
the direction, the rips, the intervals as they ready themselves.
The sun is nearly down and the new moon starts to show like a narrow rind.
I am merely watching, where once I would have entered.
I am exercising a fulsome discretion and prudence, but
I am also watching my son on his board. At twelve he is too small,
too weak yet to fight out to the break, but he rides the high seconds
near the shore. I watch him disappear again and again under
shelves of white water. I have to breathe and watch and let him
come up on his own. He is thin and graceful. Each time he emerges
there is an exultation. If I were a half mile up the beach, I could spot
him from his sheer joy. He is floating among the rushes of joy. He is
headed somewhere I have never been, to someplace I'll never set foot in.
He is practicing his spinout, his step, his stall, his rollover.
There is a star by the moon. Actually it is Jupiter, but it doesn't matter.
I can look up and down the beach. The earth pounds and shivers,
the spume rises, the waves keep roaring. There are words that cannot
abide here. There are ideas that are not possible. You can take
whatever air you want in your mouth and twist it however you like,
you will never make *sorrow,* or *confusion,* or *gloom* or their
hundred dreary comrades. A longboarder in the outside break
is carving down the face of something enormous. He is the only one
in the wave, and he is walking up, driving up the shoulder to spin
and come down again. The spray shines in the dusk. He is doing
impossible things. He looks like he will stay up forever, powering

through close-outs higher than his head. All at once the crowd
understands something. All at once we are all watching the same thing.
Even my son has rolled from his board and stands in the shallows to watch.
Now every one of us knows exactly why we've come here.
And we are all whooping and shouting like fools.

Shook Foil

I praised rope. I praised wire and the rows of clamps
and the spools of tape and the shelves of nails. I praised
the wood scraps in their discord under the bench, and I looked upon
all the paint cans, their dollops and splatters, and the brushes
hardened in the long-evaporated thinner, and the wooden barrel
filled with drop cloths. I gloried in the spiders and earwigs, the kick-out holes
of the festering termites. I honored the boxes and boxes
under the grit, the slow entropy and sprawl of things:
I stood in the silence of balled-up aluminum and flattened cardboard,
in smashed cans all bright in the bins, and the bottles guarding their fragile
    natures.
I stepped into the shadows in the cool of the morning, the concrete
razed and cracked under my feet, I minded the hooks, I minded
the runners of ivy pushing through the old roof, and the hornet's nest
under the dry eaves where the rakes hang. I stood in the great clutter.
I lifted no hand toward mere order or design, but turned a path
where the tied bags of rags parted from the rusted wagon and
the shovels and the cans of rose spray. I went back and made
myself a place for two minutes or five or for the whole hour. Then
for a time there was no time. I let the perpetual dusk
in there soothe my eyes, even while the sunlight made
its small shaft from the cracked window, oblique and mote-filled.
I praised rope. I praised the jars of wing nuts and washers
and the blades for clipping and chopping. I praised the hoses,
their stiff coils, I praised the watering can. I watched the fine dust circling.
I praised its abundance. I watched how it drifted,
I watched how it settled and covered.

Part of What I Mean

I can't keep my verbs straight. That's part of
what I mean by ecstasy. Tonight, for instance, driving
the late streets in my Jeep, not a star in the low sky,
nothing but the hunchbacked streetlights, no traffic
to speak of, and my American vernacular laying down
tracks in my head, going off on everything. I want
to shout and so I do. I want to beat drum shuffles on
the steering wheel and so I do. I want to drive in
silence down the wide lanes and so I do. I see two
police cars hulking in shadows like lazy animals:
I can't seem to find any perspective, anything to help me.
Perhaps my tenses are all wrong. I mean I was giddy, I was
terrified, I was transported at all the randomness, all
the connections, all the persistence. The government
has lined all the rivers here with cement. Perhaps you've
seen them. That way when rainy season comes, the
water won't meander and flood the housing developments.
The other eight months of the year the cement rivers
are nearly dry. If you look at them at dawn, or just when it's
getting dark, you will attest that they are impossible. They
are more arrogant than the pyramids. There has never been
a wonder like these. They give off a single musical note
that never varies or stops. If you go down in one and follow
it long enough, you come upon the metropolitan camps
of ducks and egrets, herons, muskrats, possums, skunks,
all squatting in the reeds just before the cement meets
the ocean tides. Some of the smaller flood canals that
feed into the rivers are overgrown with oleander and
ivies of every description. They are as beautiful as
the canals on Mars, but they are not rusting or often
mistaken for what they are not. I pull off onto a sidestreet
and cruise into a neighborhood I don't know. Some kids
are hanging out in a front yard, a man in shorts is sawing

something in his garage under a brilliant white light. I
stop in a cul-de-sac and get out and lean against a fender.
It's humid. The sky is socked in with overcast. All my verbs
are lining up along the sidewalk like dominoes—verbs I guess
because everything is moving and flowing. Verbs for awhile
until they change their clothes. I don't want them to impede
my thinking, which is dangerous now with every kind
of exultation: All over the rivers, all over the canals, all over
the east side, a million frogs are shrieking. Their voice is constant
in pitch, maybe like the background music of the Big Bang
or the insistent hallelujahs of an uncaused Steady State—
I am certain the proper equations could reveal something.
Let me try to tell you what kind of night it is. I am standing here,
a stranger under a streetlamp, nearly midnight, listening
to frogs in the middle of the city. No one bothers me.
No one thinks it's a bit suspicious. A police car rolls by,
and I nod and wave. One of the officers waves back.
I make no claims for this. I understand the passing
of a moment. No one knows where any of this is headed.
That's part of what I mean.

Honokaa Town, Geckos Chirping, Deep Night, No Telescope

Well, certainly the poetry of Earth is not dead, and I am
still wandering companionless among stars—I am still
appareled in celestial light: these one-eyed queens
of heaven are throwing necklaces to the crowds—they
glitter at our feet. They rattle and flash above our heads.
And I am still climbing up on coffee, and I am still climbing
down on bourbon, though the night here arches like a cat,
and the familiar guide stars are crowded and shouldered
by a thousand smaller lights in the lava blackness, in
the island loneliness. I am taking stock of what I love.
I am driven to the simple declarative. I am watching
Cassiopeia with her heirloom clusters and Andromeda
with her blurry jewel, how they take the truth and scatter it
on the sea of photons, how they are mindless of any such
thing as beauty. You can ask any star to solve your day
with its imperial candle, you can compass your hands
over the whole sky in dumb amazement, you can think
about amending your life with such precision and resolve
that you will become your own staunch beacon, regal and
peculiar, but it does no good. Here the stars and the galaxies
talk to one another along the grids of space. They are so
practical. They are so moral and willing. They have
a language all their own, though they keep their poems
filed away in the most secret places. They have every opportunity.
I, on the other hand, have only their light.

Delta Scuti

I am flexing those ancient muscles of truth and beauty.
I am looking for a *pulsing variable,* thinking that what
the old poets sang us in their sweet measures might be
right as well as wrong. I have the star atlas open on
my knees, the most sacred of texts, the one map of heaven.
Next to me is the telescope and the whirlwind and the burning bush.
All around me the desert quartz and sandstone spark
and brood in the quiet flint of starlight. The sky is a lake of ice.
You need patience and the faith that you can trace your way
back each night to the same distant tiny lantern hidden
among the magnitudes and the seas of broken worlds.
You must keep track, you must sketch and remember:
does this star bloom and die and bloom again, unlike
our own? You must be precise and say nothing of violence
and upheaval on a scale that can only be declared
in the strip-searched parlance of numbers. Here all
metaphor can only reduce, and therefore lie, though
this star is beautiful, like the cut glass on the pendent
of the young wife, seen against her bare throat through
a curtained window half a city block away. This is how
I can manage the engines of dread, how I get to keep
on saying that the rumble in the night is only a train,
that the shaking in the woodwork is a common beetle,
that what steals my daily breath is the air trying to
get back to where it belongs. *Star, star,* if I have to sleep
among the thorns I will not sleep. If I have to lie
on the bare rock, I will stand upright and keep a vigil. I know
there are things you will never tell me about your world, but
listen to me: here the scorpion's feet are rustling in the *Indian
Paintbrush,* and a cold breeze is moving in the shadow of the junipers.

North

Here lie the sectors of the Dragon and
the regions of the Great Bear. Here are the
potent nuclear angels *Giansar* and *Thuban, Sziban,*
Kuma, Rastaban, and *Arrakis,* jealous in their magnitudes.
Here are all the left hands of God, fierce in their right ascensions.
When I walk out and stand under them, even in the earliest
moments when I can still believe in my own innocence, I can
understand nothing but the dread of their holy light. Even
in the hot evenings of July, they make a shadow fall on my books,
and my eyes wander from one thin wall to another. I don't know
what I mean by holy, but I can parse dread in a hundred ways.
I don't know what calls me to say this, but a thousand billion particles
are dancing outside my window, and some of them are hailing me.
We are going north together. The common people lining
the streets will mistake our convulsions for revelry. I will
revel in my fashion. I will march untouched between the
yellow eye of *Kochab* and the red eye of *Merak.* In this
way I rejoice in my failures at love and celebrate my failures
of will. In this way I can fly from my plentiful disasters.
Now it is my own heart which will be the heart of terror
and my own breast which will be the wheel of sky.

Barnard 352

You must beware looking to the heavens in search of peace—
that is the message the stars broadcast nightly, that is
the news that swells the channels and buckles the airwaves.
Or I have simply roamed too far from the familiar stops.
Think of *The Swan*, all propriety and aloof grace, like struck
crystal over the roof and driveway, marking the direction
in which all the stars in our galaxy are traveling at reckless
speed for reasons they keep to themselves. And within
The Swan's deep pools of light and refraction lie the dark
shadows that look like emptiness but are not. Think
of *Barnard 352*, that fingernail of blackness against
the galactic dazzle, thought to be nothingness until
Barnard raised his eyes and understood: dust. And
more dust: *Barnard 361*, or *Barnard 168*. I can
sing to myself at the eyepiece and gather a certain
kind of strength. Among the forests of stars are the veiled
kings and queens that raise their arms and shout against
the silence until their voices become the silence. When
I spy one, I stop whining to God for instructions,
I stop asking for the usual things. I can rub my
knuckle or whistle a little scale, but sooner or later
my head grows heavy and my mind so weary that
all my bright thoughts and my dull thoughts crowd
one another and I want to close my eyes. But I
can't. *Oh, Lord,* I want to say, *Oh, Lord,* and then dust to
blot out a million suns, dust running in rivers and capillaries,
on its way from one happiness, on its way to one happiness.

The Lilies of the Field

One of those early summer days, driving west on
Carson Street, heading for parts unknown, singing
aloud in my head, saying *Lord, Lord, what am I to do?*
Not a heaviness in my heart, not a lightness in my heart,
but the usual hum and rush of living in this city of bungalows
and smokestacks and barges and ocean. I was trying
to keep my promises, but I didn't know how—I wasn't
expecting a sign, exactly. I wasn't expecting the family
on the parkway strip, right there on Carson Street,
the old pickup truck, and the blankets spread
in a row on the grass—and they were selling their things,
everything, from the look of it, the quick backward-rolling look
you get from a motoring car, the one way to see the world
at this hour in our century, the *elect* way because the dimension
of time doesn't allow you a single chance to delude yourself:
this is the universe expanding—shirts, pants, a child's
car-seat, bright plastic things strewn like a rummage
sale, but right there on the parkway grass, the traffic
swooshing by, and that family—five, six of them, kids,
everyone, out on the grass selling things no one would
ever want to buy. You had to ask yourself, you had
to feel things: how did they come to this? All this
in an instant, in the passing shot, in the frame of
a car window. You had to consider how much of the
Sermon on the Mount was ambiguous. You had to
at least entertain the idea that the Buddha was clearer
in his communications. You had to marvel at the
enormous figure of the angel Gabriel giving shorthand
to Mohammed. I don't think that family spoke English well.
You could get a sense of that by the look of them. We've
all been there: you nod and smile and point, you pull out
a few words, they pull out a few words, there is a little
embarrassment, those small laughs that are accompanied

by a quick forward jerk of the head. It's how to get along.
You can buy a pair of shoes that way for a dollar and a half.
You can get a Webster's dictionary for fifty cents. You
can get a King James Bible for nothing if you don't mind
the inked inscription inside the front cover: *Presented to*
Bruce Stoltley by the North Long Beach Presbyterian Church,
September 29, 1958. I know that the dangerous thing is believing
that you love everyone, every suffering thing, even while
you know you would tear out someone's lungs or step on
a person's heart in the right hour of the right day. How
the sun sits so high these days, so different from its low,
pale winter path—how everything is exfoliated in the light,
how everything begs to mean something other than itself.
I am not talking about the problem of meaning one thing,
but the truth about meaning all things, all at the same time.
Behold the lilies of the field, for instance. *Behold the birds.*
Behold the tattered colors of worldly possessions spread
out on the city green, their sudden speed, backward
in the side window of the automobile. How they vanish,
but never really vanish. How they persist. How *everything* toils.

What Good Are the Stars

I apologize to the names of my failures
    after all this time with so little to say
    now that my yard and arbor are bursting
        with orange and lemon,
with St. John's bread and the bird of paradise:
        I apologize, Paolo, though I do not use
your true name nor the names of the others—
    forgive me for only shaking my head when I heard,
        knowing the heart attack, so called,
            in the crumpled newsclipping
    could only have been heroin at forty,
        and then that very truth
reaching me by rumor and gossip,
        how you nodded off
on that scuffed couch in Connecticut:
    I am sorry for my years of silence, my old sweet partner,
        my companion evil one, but I was breathless
        then myself from my own trials,
    and before you there was Francesca,
heroin, yes, but a seizure, she is gone over, and Chico—
    I am vamping the names—Chico at the top of his crooked stairs,
fifty, hemorrhaging from his wine-scarred liver,
        and then Saint Sebastian,
you know who I mean, at forty-nine, listening to rock and roll,
    whisky bottle on the seat of his truck, vacuum cleaner
    hose taped from exhaust to window, and his note,
There are squirrels in my roof... and you, Guillermo,
    I know you can hear me, Guillermo, under your barrow
        of roots and tubers,—do you
    remember Jimi, how good he got on the guitar,
        gigs in Boston and everything?
I'm telling you I ran into him on a wharf in San Francisco,
    two particles colliding in an afterlife, and he already

had that look of an old bluesman,
but he was only painting houses then.
                    Oh, how he remembered you, Guillermo,
                    how he held you in his arms and tried to sing
the breath back into you and begged the others
                    to call the rescue squad—but they didn't
                    because the dope
and paraphernalia sat scattered all over the house,
                    and anyway they thought you would make it.

He is so sad, Guillermo, he loved you, I can tell,
                    and *you* were sad, always, and so skinny
                                and so quiet and strange,
            and I want to tell you that something strange
                        is happening now with me—
how the days shorten and the nights shorten in
            their sweaty blooms, how the lawn trembles,
and my cherry tree, and the sweet gum
                    and the white birch bent under city grit—
            how they are restless in the dark,
            how the muscles of my throat have grown sore
                            with these requiems,
                how my whole thinking is different, so that I sit up
hours at night just trying to get used to it, this
                        deep shaking
            like I must be just inches away from God,
                    and I don't feel lonely for any of you anymore
because, after all, you are here at the table
            with your robbers' eyes and your jailhouse tattoos,
and we clink our glasses in our shy way,
                    and we're all talking like in the old days,
                                and *I'm* talking,
                I'm saying, *tell me*, because I think you know and
                    I think I have forgotten:
                                    tell me,
what was the use of all our sorrows when

we roamed the Earth among its gray cities
      and shining automobiles,
        under the simple stars and the pocked moon,
all gravity and speed, coming and going?

III

This Small Book of Days

---

i was talking to a moth

the other evening

he was trying to break into

an electric light bulb

and fry himself on the wires

DON MARQUIS, *archy and mehitabel*

What angel will teach an angel? What angel will teach a man

or a woman?

SAINT AUGUSTINE

This Small Book of Days

                                        Remember
                    First to possess his books, for without them
                    He's but a sot, as I am, nor hath not
                    One spirit to command.
                                        —Caliban, *The Tempest*

On the last day it may well come to the father,
                some flaw or weakness thrust out upon
        the world, making its tight nest there,
    waiting for the dissociated voice, crying,
                as you would expect, *Father, Father,* and
        then only the brown river, the riffle
above the cupped rocks, small fish
                gliding from the little caves, and my
        violent nature flying about my head
    like a hive of stars, and still—who would dream it?—
I lick my long teeth
            and begin to see that I too might cause
    the sun and moon to part and bear
                a map of my creation on the waters,

                as on the second day
    when there were devices to engage the mind,
            a quaint device wanting the name *mind,*
                    wind over the wind-carved dune, lichen,
    places where water comes up sweet, limestone
            hollowing its breast to water, wild trellises
    where the audacious berries cluster
            and sleep while I gather them, heaping them
in my hands, all of them to my liking and pleasure,
            eating my way into language, which
    is the second power and the strictest secret

and the degree denied me until my tongue became muscle,
          and I broke the marrow bone of *names,*

      thus wild things on the third day
I came to know by manipulating their terms
        and finding my way to invention: *small bear that*
            scuttles by swamps, the whine and suck of the
    dizzy flies, the lips of this island making it
by my newfound logic a *mouth,* and what it swallows,
        assiduous bee, skunk, skunkflower, cosmopolis rat,
     owl who feeds, drying ouzel in the sun, stinkbeetle,
earthworm, my own name, my own form, shaggy and shaking
    behind me like a shadow, terror from which I run

            until the fourth day,
    and the goad without mercy, which is *desire,*
and one desires only beauty and completeness,
    at night the frogs shrieking for sex,
turning the sky into a chorus of hunger, each thing
    aching to bring its own kind into this place,
        each thing taking its measure of me
    whether I am its sovereign, as was promised, or whether
      I am to be deposed, cast out, sent into the heart
of an oak to be alone and uncompleted in this ruined lust
  by which we are both mocked and come to God,

         but on the fifth, we question this:
for if God, then why? It is no different
    than waking and feeling the father's face receding,
        the lore of all the books coming to nothing.
    Who spun the first particle on its end
  and said, *moon* or *angel* or *number?* Who drinks
the tide and gives it back, what sets the shellfish
    to such comforts, loafing under their mounds of solace?

What is that sound, so much like sobbing,
when the wind comes out of the southeast
and the glass falls, and the men who would be my masters
beseech me to show them some haven,
and I am so gleeful and deaf and curious?

And then six is my number and my riddle, six
is my star and six is my portion,
the sixth day is my own celebration whereby we enter
the crude city, bark-roofed hovels, animal skins,
the squalor of smoked meats, the misery of children, bread
lying on tables in the plaza,
fly-specked fruits drying on pegs at the merchants' booths,
the riot of vegetables, the jugs of commerce:
stiff-lipped, grinning, I walked
the sixth day among them and tasted their blight, smelled
their women and jostled their men,
and none was the wiser, six
tending toward balance and repose, six my ruler,
six my charm, six my strangeness,

remembering then the first day,
remembering therefore a terrible time when I was nothing,
and so composing on my black drum all manner
of plaintive elegies for whatever it was
that locked me to this island and then disappeared,
as if on the first day a book had opened
and then suddenly closed again
and left me in my rags by the river
among the fish and the lights in the sky, thinking
how something surely must have moved me on the first day
and then locked me to this island
and on my drum, the skin pulled taut as night,
in the brave language of the book,
all manner of plaintive elegies—

Lines Written Against the Day
This Hand Will Tremble

Tremble not for the first time, but tremble without
horizon, like the oranges on my mandarin tree breaking
down their own limbs under their mindless weight, or
the sweet gum weeping its yellow leaves, knowing only
that it is time to weep. I am astonished that it took me
this long to discover how the spirit addresses the flesh,
how the flesh addresses the spirit, how peculiar this is,
how unfinished, how happy with the crows sitting on
the electric wires, so pure and out of proportion, and
the wires drooping each so mathematically, and the
utility poles full of carpenter bees and termites, not a one
thinking it might be a tree or a statue. And I am out
for the long afternoon, with the sun shortening its track,
and I am walking the orderly pavements among parked
cars until the dusk comes and Venus shines as big as a
bottle-cap in the south. I am avoiding familiar turns
as if I had a choice in the matter. Sometimes I think
I do. It is the same as thinking that the spirit is a name
for the flesh. Or the other way around. And I am out
among the heedless streets watching the lights come on
in the windows and doorways. One thing speaks to another,
or else I am speaking to myself. Now there is room:
infinite, abundant room for all my weeping and trembling.

A Witness Gives His Version

> I am someone other than an "I" of whom I do not know if he exists. . . .
> —Fernando Pessoa

I don't know how I know this,
but if simple presence could hover
in a room unseen, then I was
the one who watched that tenderest
labor as the woman, her head bound
in a white kerchief, silently bent
over the corpse, washing it with
a fistful of cloth that she dipped
into an enameled basin and wrung
dripping with both raw hands.
Others were in that room. I saw them.
Some were neighbors, clearly come
to proffer aid and experience.
One man lingered, dressed in gray
wool pants that hung from leather braces.
He looked dazed and immeasurably sad
as only a man could look who would not
be permitted to weep in his station
as man in this tiny house of rough boards.
Against the back wall, by the doorway
to another room, stood the iron stove,
and upon it the copper utensils. I
was nowhere, I was nothing, for there was
no *I* yet to bear witness, and still
I was present when they wrapped the body
in the winding cloth, swaddling the limbs
and tying the jaw.

It's enough, you might say, for me
to tell you this—the way someone

might speak of a dream over coffee,
dreamily pensive, touching on some
useful meaning as though every tale
were allegory and bore upon a life.
But these other lives—*their* lives—
they could never have known me among them.
Would we say they are merely vocabulary,
this gaunt dead woman and her ministers?
It might do, for the other explanations
are tedious, and yet I might go farther
and tell you that I remember another
door behind me, and that I knew what
lay beyond it, the dark, pre-electric
village street, the gray ocean water,
never far, the other board houses,
the picket fences, the winter-dead roses
on the fine trellises: and suddenly
because there was no *I*, I became
the angel or the ghost, and I was moved
by their sorrow and their mortal plight.
And because they might have sensed me
there or thought, even fleetingly, that
they were not alone, I fled until I came
to this convenient place of forgetting,
before they might have imputed something
untoward to me, wisdom or power
or the smallest ability to intervene.

Moon by Night

I am breathing *moon, moon,* and I can't pull
myself from it, *moonstruck,* as in the stories
of lovers or murderers, though I still claim
that I am harmless and believe it, I still claim
reason when it suits me, I claim to thirst for
righteousness—it's the moon's loneliness
that draws me, its utter, bereft isolation that
convinces me it is pure and cleansed:
I can pass from the *Sea of Cold*
over the *Taurus Mountains,* along the edges
of the *Marsh of Sleep* and thereby, if I am
resolute and not given to wandering,
come with safety and great wonder to
The Sea of Fertility: here the escarpments
seem cut from chalk, and the sun's shadows
show the ridges and rifts in blazed relief. I
can weary the long journey south, if south were
ever in the moon's compass, although I must
gently urge the telescope *up,* away from all
intuition, for the mirrors baffle light and nothing
stands upright according to the ordinary laws,
and therefore it isn't merely *wonder,* it isn't
merely *anything* one says it is: whatever I declare
keeps me watching can't be counted upon—
righteousness, after all, can mean salvation
or good conduct, or power or will, or the law—
nothing is simple, no landscape, no vision: there
is no such thing as a surface, only infinite depths,
only what I covet, what I wish I could love:
this is what I see, this is what I hear in the air
around my head on such a clear and explicit night,

and why should I doubt it? Others have been
here. Others have watched. Others have struck
names on the white rock: *Serenity. Tranquillity.
The Sea of Nectar. The Lake of Dreams.*

Nox Erat et Caelo

I'm trapped in the house when all I want
is to hear Latin—any Latin, but I must be drunk
again on the liquor of the priests of my dreamtime—
that's what must be at me, brain and funk, this hot night,
this night when the moon was shining in a cloudless sky,
which is true, though I appropriated that line's whole
cloth from Horace. The moon, of course, is so scrolled
with Latin you can study it like a text, but it is utterly silent
in its coming and going, all the more so through the barrel
of a telescope when the sheer velocity of its transit
makes your breathing so shallow that you can hear the blood
pound in your head. I don't remember when the priests
stopped singing. Maybe I was already long gone by then.
I don't remember the year all Gaul was divided
into three parts. What's wrong with the earth that I
cannot run into the streets and hear Latin at this hour?
What did my mother do with my little black Latin
prayer book that I bought with my own money? I suspect
that the world was never better than it is now, even
with all its evil and despair and cruelty. But if this very
moment surpasses anything that came before it, I am
guilty, then, of the worst offenses, of chasing after
a sweetness that was never there, or after a moment
that flexes in beauty simply because it was mine once.
Where are the sentences? Where are the moods, the tenses,
the declensions, the cases? All through the rooms the clocks
tick and the lamps burn with easeful light. I shuffle through
a few books. I listen at the window. I pour myself
another cup of coffee. I permit myself anything and everything,
but tonight it is Latin I solicit, Latin profound under moonlight or
immured in my quiet walls, Latin before the dulcet streaks of morning.

I Am Refused Entry to the Harvard Poetry Library

Rightly so: for who am I but a tired question
squatting, in those days, somewhere up on
Beacon Hill, snow equally tired, crusted and dirty,
crouching in striated piles along the ancient curbs—
such a homely winter. And so there should
be books at my elbow! And there were rumors
of that splendid room: imagine sitting in
the warm, thick air, among the sons and daughters
of the sons and daughters, among the thin spines,
among the soft chairs. I would not eat all
day but linger there and let the gray light slant
through the gothic windows, or the square windows,
or from brass lamps, or from fluorescent lights,
the exact details so impossible to imagine
that they roll and flicker and agitate
the manic breath and heart: walk to the T and lay
my coins down, count the stops, hunch in
the chill morning to coffee and sugar at the vendor's
cart near the square, then advance, certain I can
talk my way into the sanctified places, sure
I can find in my pocket some scrap of card,
some guarantee I might pass. And if the world
has its own ideas, and if they are not in accord
with my own wishes, and if the mild young woman
shakes her head firmly and explains how I in
general never have, and never will, live a qualified
day in my life, I must not be afraid of the cold gray
sky and the sprawling yard—I must walk among
the gay colors of the coats and scarves, the backpacks
of the deserving: there are other buildings open
for roaming, and though I might be regarded
with the sideways look reserved for my kind,
someone will soon lay down a book or some other
thing that will fit a hand, and swiftly it will be mine.

February

My stepfather coming home
from the wharves to draw his unemployment
and smoke Pall Malls in the sagging
overstuffed wing-chair, cheeks softening
with a beard that grew brindled now,
his life getting on, going nowhere,
sometimes a listless game of checkers
that I never wanted to play with him,
but mostly his drinking coffee from
a chipped bowl and brooding and sending
me once a week down to the boats
with a bucket to ask the luckier men
for flounder or haddock, and always
their wind-darkened faces staring
away from me at the wet decks
as they hoisted the brimming bucket back,
those weeks of fish and eggs and onions
and only cold water running in the taps,
the sun never getting above the line
of the woodshed roof, starlings flapping
down to croak on the crusty backyard snow,
the dank walls muttering to one another
when they thought no one listened, hats
and scarves awake on a nail by the door,
but nothing to dress for and no place to go.

Whiskey

Which is foolish to praise
for it took my grandfather's
sopping life and wrung it out
like the old checkered shirt
he always wore, wool sluffed down
to a sheen of green threads,
but still it comes more or less
directly from God, one of the great
charms against the several forms
of pain and the one nostrum
for ague that really works,
taken with the juice of a
sour fruit, heated in pewter
over a candle flame: of course
it makes you dream—it takes
you down into the vegetable soul,
but look, it makes you also
resemble the spirit, which it is,
in that you will think you are your
essences and so recite the sadness
of the body. It is not metaphor.
It does not need us. Neither is it
pleasure in the same way that a man
or woman might be comfort to the other,
or in the way a small child might run
to you, glad for your face or voice,
and yet its acids will bathe you.
And it *sings*. Take it down quickly
in the small glass. There is Ulysses
tied to his weathered pole, and there,
in the sun that is setting among
the strong fires of the vanishing world,
are its voices, so sweet, so naked. All

is not well, but no bell is struck,
and the watch sleeps, forsaken. The
oracle says, *you will die alone
raving in a squalid room, and none
shall weep,* and you nod and smile,
for that will not be today when
the wind is in your hair, and the sea
breaks likes diamonds under your
fine ship, rocking, plundering forth.

Dream Talk

Around the kitchen, always with
an edge to it, coffee and scowling,
and this was when we heard about
the new job, or maybe his becoming
foreman, or how we'd all live up
in that big apartment on top of
the East End Cold Storage because
then he would be the night manager—
and there was more: all those artless
contraptions of language, that speech
so simple you could spit it from
your curled mouth, and yet it was
the breath in its most divine robe,
how it washed the walls clean
and kept the cold out of your
mean coat, and how it got one
or another out of bed each morning
and off to the spiritless work, or to
no work, always with some new story
emerging, untouchable, just off in the fog,
just across the water, something
you or I could learn to make up
at a table with dishes and cigarettes
and the easy words, a spell
to carve on the poised world: meat,
potatoes, a new oil stove, an early
spring, forsythia in the garden,
the smell of lavish roses blowing
through aluminum window screens,
a bright new camera and a clean
family bunched before it, smiling
at the lens with lucky eyes.

When Lilacs

The pine fence rotted and collapsed,
and then there was nothing between us
and the abandoned lot of the fish-
packing company, its wild outbuildings,
the forges and pumps, the truck barn,
the coopery, the workshops, silent
and weedgrown, and the counting-house,
ivy-choked and gone to pigeons and
feral cats—and the lilac tree, stooped
with blossoms, and my mother stealing
among them like a ragged queen, snipping
and gathering, filling milkbottles with
the nodding clusters: she would choke
the house's sorrows with the lilacs
in the kitchen with its pinched windows,
on the sills and shelves and sinkboard,
on the red round table and the stove's back,
and lilac water in the vases and jars—
and in every cluttered room, we, who
tilled no gardens and tended nothing
but the tedious rosary of one day at a time,
suddenly rolling among the crowns
of flowers, breathing whatever fever
it was that sweetened the air for that
one time, the time the dead fence crumbled
and nothing stood between us
and the rich swollen purses of the lilacs.

Kapital

Hooking boxes of dogfish
across the packinghouse floor,
take the fat grease pencil you
use to mark **36/BOS** or **42/NY**
on the split-pine box lids
and draw a circle around
the place where *labor* becomes
surplus or where my stepfather's
cigarette, thirty cents a pack
in those days, went sparking
from his lip when his boot
hit the wet ice, when he went
under the wheels of the forklift:
three cents a pound, twenty-thousand
pounds, packed in ice and stacked:
take your allowance for boxes,
the box-makers in their wire cages
pumping pedals, take your
allowance for diesel, take
the boat's share, the owner's
two shares, the skipper's son's
half-share, take making that ripped
pair of gloves last another week,
take him hot soup and bread,
take him his worthless union card
and his thermos of coffee
and his watchcap over his ears:
you can't save him—he only
wanted to come home to a hot supper,
hash and eggs in the blackened pan
and then lean against the iron stove
to warm his back before bed.
But there's nothing you can do

in your small child's terror
when the woman says, *What
will we eat? How will we live?*
You *will* eat and you *will* live,
this time, in this life, though
in other times you have perished,
and on winter mornings thereafter
you have risen to the lunch pail
and drifted along the glazed wharves
and reckoned your wage on your fingers,
your hard eye drawing its essential light
skyward from the idle trawlers
while they locked and buckled
in the freezing harbor.

Small Prayer for the World Without Mercy on Us

> Thou hast not given water to
> the weary to drink, and thou hast
> witholden bread from the hungry.
> —Book of Job

Then they found themselves
in the usual corridors,
the backroads and oak-stands,
following the ghost ruts
of extinct wagon-roads
in yellow fields where fences
drooped their abused wires,
coming expertly to a sequestered place,
berries on shining wood swelling
like tiny apples, and a ragged
melody rising from the radio
in the farmhouse where they
spoke in the language that would
become the *old* language, and
the arrangements were made, and
of a night in distinct back-seat
Oldsmobiles they came, carrying
the signs of the chosen, the bedbug,
the headlouse, the deep lung wet
with bacilli, packing the wooden
rosary and the vigil candle
and making their way in narrow file
along the night trails that paralleled
the cataracts of light roaring *freeway*
and *pilgrim,* shuddering in the swift cold
and the swift sex of flight. And after all,
it would seem impossible to die here
among such abundance and garish blessing—
or then to die having seen a land

driven beyond any simple category of
good or evil—rising from the dusky
fields, the certain camps, the secret
pews of select churches and hanging
the familiar herbs in the windows of
walk-up, two-family kitchens, sowing
the asphalt roadways of the earth with labor,
saying nothing because God's language
is not language, and the passage
from one life to another can never
be death, and what has been withheld
counts for nothing in the mysterious
ledgers of *this* world, this place where
they themselves refuse to give up nothing.

Fortunate Rain, Lucky Star

The Winged Horse in September, in his vagrant
altitude over the pond in the park—and so much
all around him, all those radiant kilns, whose names
have been passed to me so carefully, like banked coals
wrapped in the soft hairy leaf waiting for my own breath
to blow them alive, orange and gold in the city's sky:
Fortunate Rain, in my own tongue according to the translations,
and *Lucky Star* and *Saddle* and *Nose* and *Shoulder* and *Wing*—
or, if I please to release the full incantations, *Matar, Homam,
Markab, Enif, Scheat, Algenib.* The air trembles sometimes
with their power, but it is difficult to know if it is the spell or
the giants themselves, so barrel-chested and hydrogen-greedy,
eyeing everything, even the rough boys who eye *me* and pass
in their own shadows down the long concrete rifts in darkness
where the trees become a wood and the wood lurks in the heart
of the East Side. Sometimes I grow so tired of sweeping the sky
lens after lens, signifying only an oddness in the marmoreal wastes,
and around me the paper cups and soda cans and the stagnant water
and the violent matter that has become duck and fish and crow and
owl and possum—sophisticates, urbane, so exactly mindful of
purpose and haunt. And, Dark Horse, *you* are so shy and desolate,
don't ask me how I know—but tonight, how horrible to be a star,
no matter what you might devour. What will save you this time?
Surely *I* can do nothing, dark blood, dark eye, lucky tongue of fire.

The Standard Times

Night after night my directions were sealed—
up Tremont and then Cottage and then west on Bradford,
out along the woods and marsh and then back around,
eastward on Commercial, along Provincetown Harbor,
thirty-some houses, more in summer. But the winter
is when the sky turned out its tenants, and Orion and Draco
and the Minor Bear slowly revealed their lineaments to such a one
as me, skinny, poorly kept, not quite human yet, knowing little
except that that the *Cape Cod Standard Times* paid my lunches
at school, most of the time. This was when such a creature
could dream of walking on wedged heels right up into space,
shivering, head up in the legible air, learning Mars and Jupiter
and Saturn, never knowing a day to go by when I didn't save
the phase of the moon in my memory: open the storm door
and drop the folded paper in—hunch down the walk, up the next,
hurrying only because of the cold leaking in under the thin coat,
but even that didn't diminish the stars, for the stars were
muscled beyond cold, and sinewed beyond the shabby forces
of such a threadbare story. Night after night, leaning under
the freight of the world's news in my greasy canvas shoulder-
sack, understanding one thing at a time, letting the plan of
the sky come to me, letting every other plan come to me
like figures of music against figures of music, the sky in its
ordained hieroglyphic, each pulsing star holding something
just out of reach, each of my successive footsteps growing
lighter and lighter as if I moved away from the earth, as if
the wind would ever stop its whining and finally bear me up.

Education by Stone

after Joao Cabral de Melo Neto

To go to it often, to catch its level impersonal voice,
says de Melo Neto in the graveyard's moon-white orchards.
To being hammered, the lesson in poetics, the speller of spells,
he says. What did you learn standing while the east wind guttered
over the fields of tilting stone, above the beloved dead, who
must love the stones in the field as they love the field?
As the stone loves, in turn, in its way, hardened and misunderstood:
It is not past loving. It is only past loving in one way of speaking.

So the stone teaches, and the stones teach, and you sat at their feet
and stumbled over your lessons. The stones made a catechism
for you, dense and like their hearts, resolute and singly knowing.
Who will recite like stone, like the stones? Who will bear
with compacted heart the inscriptions of the names of so much
that was beautiful? Will you? In their toppled kingdom, will you?

Confessions

> And what is this God? I asked the earth and it
> answered: "I am not he," and all things that are on
> the earth confessed the same thing.

I

Voice over:

> Then to Carthage I came.
> Shadows on the flat water
> and towers majestic in their
> darkened shoulders which
> slouched coldly from the light . . .

New voice interrupts:

> *Delusions:* Nothing but a photograph
> tacked to the corkboard of a study wall,
> an old Mentor paperback, underlined,
> its yellowed pages scaling
> like the unwaxed leaf,
> unremembered, found pressed
> and crumbling among
> yesterday's news . . .

First voice, as if from a distance:

> *And how shall I pray to my God?*
> *When I pray to him, I call*
> *Him into my self. And in me*
> *what place or room is there?*

II

Girl speaking:

> (To someone, somewhere, she might sound lost in
> the raptures of glossolalia, but WE HEAR:)

> Look, look, I know if you guys laid
> a little taste on me, I could pay you back
> because I'm going downtown later tonight
> to this bar where I know this guy, he
> buses tables there, down on Christopher Street,
> and he's out scoring right now, and
> he owes me for some things,
> and so I could like pay you tonight, late
> or even lay a little aside,
> because like, you know, you'll want
> to score again quick, but this way
> you won't have to, right away I mean,
> and you know

(Her voice begins fade-out):

> you weren't given dominion
> over the lights of heaven,
> you weren't given dominion
> over the gathering together
> of the waters . . .

III

Seeing:

> Seeing an ANGEL in standard form,
> which is to say human form, but

a power emanates here, and we are reminded
of the strangers that came to Sarah's door,
walking out of radiance and into
the clumsy apparatus of this perilous life,
but the TWO BOYS do not see this figure
who stands and watches them. The BOYS—
young men, really—stand in the shabby
room by a gas cookstove. One holds
a small device made from twisting handles
of wire around the cap of a discarded
wine bottle. It is a spoon in which
they cook down Dilaudid tablets, which
they will then shoot up. FIRST BOY
holds a spoon over the licking blue
tongues of the gas jet. The other
takes an eyedrop tube, a baby-
pacifier, a needle and an elastic
band and assembles the homemade
hypodermic. The ANGEL, although
we suspect it may be nothing but *language,*
now fills the room with an odd light,
and through it we see the GIRL
sitting on the single bed and understand
that she is the girl who before was speaking.

Seeing:

                    the city now through
          the crabbed window above the bed,
          seeing the girl's shining brown
          hair, seeing the four flights
          of stairs, the hallway bathroom,

We see:

from the boxy automobiles
in the dim street, from the
clothing and hair of the boys
that it is a time past,
we see that it is a time unlike our own.

IV

What the Angel Said

Angel:

She's that girl you followed
to the roof, nothing under
her wool skirt, so you could
look up as she stepped on
the rungs of the iron ladder
and she pushed on the trapdoor,
and you gazed up into that
unkempt bush between her legs,
that puckered crescent of skin
that was part of all your torment.

First boy:

Torment?

Angel:

You think it leads to God.

First boy:

You are talking about cruelty.

Angel:

So called. It's necessary.
But you didn't fuck that day.

First boy:

I don't remember.

Angel:

You got loaded. You shared that
screwball needle.

First boy:

In those days it meant nothing. Next to nothing.

Angel:

You think of her still. You remember
when you stole her purse?

First boy:

There were things I wanted to do
with her that we never got to.

79

Angel:

And I've put so much work into you!

First boy:

Someone already said it—aren't you just a voice?

V

The Work in Progress

CUT TO:

Exterior shot. New York, circa nineteen
sixty-something, small ethnic neighborhood
on the lower westside. WE SEE the Hotel
Manhattan sign in the distance. In the
FOREGROUND, chainlink fence, alley,
the forlorn brick of doomed walkup
buildings, smoke rising from grates in
the street. Stage left is the rear
of the Star Hotel, whorehouse. Women
black as asphalt, rough, cursing,
sit on the steps drinking wine from
bottles in paper bags. FIRST BOY
passes and they call out to him. He
calls back. They all seem to know
one another, distantly. They would
feed upon one another if it came
to that, but for now there is
some hard laughter. The BOY
throws them the finger and FIRST GIRL
yells, "*That the size of your dick?*"

CUT TO:

Cold streets, the slush and bark
of Third Avenue where the BOYS
see a BUM, an old navy drunk
who slips in the street, gashing
his face, and they lift him and
walk him to a doorway. In another
doorway a young white WOMAN, bloated,
drops her khaki pants and stares at
herself, a wild look in her eyes.

CUT TO:

BOYS walking up avenue, dark,
bent to the cold wind. Around
them the city sparkles in
abundant light. The windows
of the tall buildings shine
and shine with colors. We
realize that it is Christmas.

MORE MORE MORE MORE MORE

VI

Apologia

You could say *nothing but a voice*,
or *nothing but a roomful of voices*,
whatever it is that the self is,
uneasy detante among uncivilized
delegates, murderers and thieves
stinking of smoke and wrapped in wolfskins,
doors wide open so that any vagabond

might rummage on through, demanding board,
claiming to be the lost king.
Any number of ways to explain what
       (in this other life,
       where all things are done so
       differently, the boat that carries
       us, the boatman so steady at his
       carriage)
it might mean that one
could pick up that flaky old
book, dried glue at its spine, one
dollar and twenty-five cents in a
PX bookstore, carried in baggage,
stored in dust, brought out after
years to a civil whiskey on a night
of wildfire in the parched foothills;
that on such a night one dare
the possibility of never clearing
the rooms of those disheveled, dangerous,
and uninvited guests.
              What
can any of this have to do with *you?*
            Listen to
Augustine of Hippo, in
the year three hundred and
ninety-nine:
          The memory also
contains the innumerable
principles and laws of numbers
and dimensions. I have heard
the sounds of the words by which
these principles are signified
when we discuss them, but the
sounds and the principles are
different things.
           And elsewhere:
This same memory also contains

the feelings of my mind. There
is nothing surprising in this.
                         And elsewhere:
What then am I? What is my nature?

VII

Memory

To have in one's mind
what is *not there*—or
to assemble the pieces again
in some order. It was lovely
at times—or else, *delusion.*
But: the old Metropole
where you could press your face
against the window glass
and from the sidewalk see
Gene Krupa, legend, still alive
behind his great drums—or
the old man in Washington Square
who pedaled a vendor's cart
and wore a fez and called himself
Sharammer with a Hammer—or
on 42nd street, two hamburgers
for thirty-five cents, and your
friend, who loved you, pulling out
all the change he owned in the world
and feeding you, and your drinking
piña colada and the tough girls
coming around and the dirty-faced
hustlers who liked your earring.
What are you doing to yourself?
shrilled the woman, who had known you,
who never should have seen you,

leaving you astonished that you
could ever have been found, and aching,
wandering the long avenue among
the chestnut sellers and winter trees
cased in sudden ice, gleaming.

VIII

And If I Cried, Who'd Listen to Me?

First voice, in reprise:

Now if you will agree, for art's sake,
that the angel exists, then accept that it
somehow watched you and saved you
for something. In this way time is
destroyed, for you look back and
alter the past from the present,
this new self becoming that very
angel who slips wave-like, particle-like
among the folds of light and matter
and whose hand seems cold and cruel
in its sculpting of experience. But
you were stone and needed hard blows,
says the angel, and shall receive
them still, for your comfort was
never its concern; only the shape,
only the shapeliness, of this sliver
of radiance you call a life: and so
dance on the tip of a needle, no one
will come with a scroll written
in that first creed when sound and thing
were not so distant: *It is
not you who enlighten every man
and woman who cometh into this world!*

You are entitled to exactly nothing
(and you think, as on nights like this,
crowded with the dead faces from
a gone world, about those others:
those ghosts that come in out of the weariness,
whatever became of them, and what angel
ever touched their lives, whether they
flourished or perished, having nothing
to do with you and your comfortable inventions,
which save, ultimately, nothing).
And yet you dreamed once, in the long,
slow, dripping narcotic dream,
that exact scroll drifting above
the rolling sea in cinematic cliché,
the voice-over in a brute language
and in it all the secrets,
and as you nodded and scratched
you knew you would wake soon
and leave that world and its splendors,
and you would come back to *this* world,
and the angel would say from your mouth
that you were lucky,
that it was fortune to return,
here, imperfect, befuddled,
carrying your simple weight down
the avenues of light and noise,
and because your angel watched
and favored you, you would
carry that weight for a while yet,
and be dumb and walk among the living,
becoming certain that we bless
and receive blessing
even as we devour one another
and are devoured,
even as, against all evidence,
you cannot stop burnishing the idea
that something beyond these walls of firmament,

a thing between memory and invention,
seems implacable,
seems to shine.

The Brittingham Prize in Poetry

The University of Wisconsin Press Poetry Series
Ronald Wallace, General Editor

Places/Everyone • Jim Daniels
C. K. Williams, Judge, 1985

Talking to Strangers • Patricia Dobler
Maxine Kumin, Judge, 1986

Saving the Young Men of Vienna • David Kirby
Mona Van Duyn, Judge, 1987

Pocket Sundial • Lisa Zeidner
Charles Wright, Judge, 1988

Slow Joy • Stefanie Marlis
Gerald Stern, Judge, 1989

Level Green • Judith Vollmer
Mary Oliver, Judge, 1990

Salt • Renée Ashley
Donald Finkel, Judge, 1991

Sweet Ruin • Tony Hoagland
Donald Justice, Judge, 1992

The Red Virgin: A Poem of Simone Weil • Stephanie Strickland
Lisel Mueller, Judge, 1993

The Unbeliever • Lisa Lewis
Henry Taylor, Judge, 1994

Old & New Testaments • Lynn Powell
Carolyn Kizer, Judge, 1995

Brief Landing on the Earth's Surface • Juanita Brunk
Philip Levine, Judge, 1996